W9-ADX-826

Virtuoso Literature for Two and Four Hands

By Diane Wakoski

DIANE WAKOSKI

Virtuoso
Literature
for Two
and Four
Hands

Doubleday & Company, Inc.
Garden City, New York
1975

MIDDLEBURY COLLEGE LIBRARY

3/1975
Am. Lit.

The poems "Walking Past Paul Blackburn's Apt. On 7th St." and "A Poem With A Blackburnian Warbler's Beginning" reprinted by permission of *Lakes and Prairies*, Copyright © 1974 by Lakes and Prairies; "The Story Of Richard Max-field," *Poetry*, Copyright © 1973 by the Modern Poetry Association; "The Emerald Essay," *The American Poetry Review*; "Winter Sequences," published by Black Sparrow Press; "To The Young Man Who Left The Flowers On My Desk One April Afternoon," *Coastlines*, used by permission; "On Seeing Two Goldfinches Fly Out Of An Alder Tree" also appears in Perishable Press chapbook as "The Wandering Tatler."

Copyright © 1973, 1975 by Diane Wakoski
All Rights Reserved
Printed in the United States of America
First Edition

Library of Congress Cataloging in Publication Data

Wakoski, Diane.
   Virtuoso literature for two and four hands.

   Poems.
   I. Title.
PS3573.A42V5   813'.5'4
ISBN 0-385-00532-6
ISBN 0-385-00463-X pbk.
Library of Congress Catalog Card Number 74-12718

PS
3573
A42
V5

this book is dedicated to the snake
in the garden, for he offered the
taste of knowledge, without which I
would rather not live

Preface

I studied the piano for fifteen years but did not become a pianist. Still, I developed a love for keyboard literature which is very deep.

I started writing poems when I was quite young. I remember a poem about a rose bush which I wrote when I was seven. I hope I have become a poet. At any rate my love for poetry is also deep.

In this book of poems, I am trying to explore the images of fantasy and my past. My keyboard now is the typewriter. The inevitable garden of my youth and innocence (Southern California covered with flowers), my pursuit of beauty and love, which to me are represented by music and flowers, my search for a poetry that can be lived—I have attempted to put these things together in this collection of poems.

I would like to thank Blanche Hillhouse, who taught me how to play the piano, and Tanya Ury, who taught me I could never be a pianist. I would like to thank Shakespeare and the brothers Grimm for teaching me to write poetry, and Thomas Parkinson for giving me faith that I could be a poet.

DIANE WAKOSKI

Contents

Pools Of The Bright And Irradiating Sun

When you are young and standing in the sunshine,
you do not think about what it is like
when the sun does not shine.

When you are young and it is dark,
and the rain pours down like flames eating the
crumpled newspaper under that split log,
you do not remember what it was like
to have sun on your bare & slightly freckled
shoulder

When you are young,
the world is an ocean
and you do not dream of any reason
for counting all the fish.

But when you are not young,
there is never sun without the memory of
a wet day in the rain,
the slick water running off your hand
as if it were sheet metal.
And counting,
we are always counting
as we grow older,
an act of remembrance,
an act of love,
how many triggers,
angels,
or Emperors
swam in this sea,

their stripes and colours,
                    shapes
rising and greeting
a stray beam of light,

how many,
we count them,
as if it proved
experience,
as if it were possible
to love
more than once,
as if experience existed
purely
without memory.

I wonder if we're ever young.
That is, innocent?
Memory destroys the past.
Or creates one.
The human embryo
goes through a gill stage.
Yet some,
like me,
never learn to swim.

The Story Of Richard Maxfield

He jumped out of a window.
Or did he shoot himself?
Was there a gun,
or was it pills?
Did anyone see blood?
Was he holding water in his lungs?
Or was he right about the CIA conspiracy and killed by one
of them
because he knew their plan?

Richard was an electronic composer.
He wrote a piece called "Cough Music" made up of the coughs
of hundreds of people at concerts.
He was brilliant and well organized.
And then he fell apart.
He was homosexual and took drugs.
He was brilliant and well organized.
I loved "Cough Music" and could not see how such a fine
composer could fall apart as Richard fell apart.

That is the story of Richard Maxfield.
He died in California.
It did not make me as sad that he died
as that he fell apart.
We all die.
We do not all fall apart.
"Cough Music" was a beautiful piece of music.

                              I went to a
concert tonight
and heard many people coughing,
especially during the encore which was a piano piece by
Debussy, delicate and sparse,
like a dress you can see through,
and everyone seemed to have to cough
during this piece.

If you cough very hard,
do you think you fall apart?
I once had a bad cough
and now realize that for two weeks I coughed during every
poetry reading and concert I went to.
I wonder if anyone recorded my cough?
I wonder how many readers and performers
not only did not feel sympathetic towards
my bad lungs and the symptomatic cough
but also wanted to shoot me for coughing?
A fortuneteller once said I would die of TB. I wonder if that's
why I like "Cough Music"?
                         Perhaps I should have my lawyer
write into my will,
                    "I would like to have 'Cough Music' played
                    at my funeral."

Someone would think that in bad taste.
No one likes to think that after you die you still have
bad taste.
Even if you had it in life.

What bothered me the most about Richard Maxfield was that
he had the bad taste to fall apart;
dying after you fall apart is actually a rectification
of bad taste.
Richard was so brilliant and well organized
I could not imagine how he fell apart.
And "Cough Music" is just one of his very beautiful concrete
tapes.
They say the men he loved destroyed him.
But he was brilliant and well organized and I find it hard
to believe some not-brilliant and poorly organized man could
destroy him.

You see, the story of Richard Maxfield is one I do not
understand.
But I have always loved "Cough Music"
and when I heard the beautiful Debussy tonight
and thought of a man I love
who for many reasons I cannot see or be with
and I heard the audience coughing, flashing every once in a while
like light catching a strip of aluminum which blows on a fruit
tree,

I understood that I would never fall apart,
though I did not know why,
and for a moment I thought of the involuntary action of
coughing, and I understood perhaps
why he jumped out of a window,
though I knew that just as I would never fall apart,
I would also never jump out of a window,
and I also refrained from coughing, though just at the end of the
Debussy,
                    I wanted to/   maybe just to join the whole crowd.

There are many ways to die,
but none of them is subtle.
                                Why *do* people cough so much
at concerts?

I cannot touch the piano.
I cannot touch you.
If the King of Spain gave a concert
no one would cough.
The story of Richard Maxfield is one I do not understand,
but I thought of it tonight,
listening to people cough their way through Debussy,

It was not music.

Only Richard Maxfield made music out of coughing, and he is dead.
Richard Maxfield is dead.

Second Chance

for Lauren, who once played the violin

No moon tonight.
And so these words will be my moon,
like bright silver dimes a blackened railroad engineer
put into the toes
of a new little pair of red shoes
he bought for his daughter.
That image,
from a novel I read
this summer.
I am fascinated by the small shoes
children wear,
the shoe/   a protection against rock,
our lives/   the shoes of children
seeming so innocent and small to me,
and though he did not mean for her to walk with dimes under
her toes,
I think of the silver there,
making trails,
like comets at dawn.

Two days ago,
I almost killed myself,
A terrible experience, current vaulting out of the desk lamp
I held in my hand,
every nerve buzzing, whirring, charging through me,
as if I were a house in which someone were ringing the doorbell,
until I fell back on the floor,
almost sure I was nearly dead,
and happily unplugged the lamp,
lay trembling and weeping,
afraid I still might die.
I was barefooted,
innocent against all the volts of my lamp,
and falling over,
giving in,
was what unplugged the lamp/
saved me.
Michael says it could not have killed me.
Not enough current in a small desk lamp,
and I defer to his knowledge of electric appliances.
I know I thought I was dying,
and it made me angry.

Angry and more frightened
than I have ever been.
I slept wearing my rubber-soled sandals that night.
Today,
two days later,
I am barefooted again.
It is summer, after all.

In my mind,
the moon hangs in the sky,
full,
like a girl with silver dimes hidden
in the toes of her slippers,
excited with the secret silver at her tips,
the moon,
simple in a telescope,
a very white lacy slip,
the white sheets of a hospital.

If I had a secret loving father,
who had slipped dimes in the toes of my shoes,
what would have happened when I picked up that lamp?
I am fascinated
by the small shoes
little children wear.

No moon tonight,
but a friend writes from a place called
"Silver Sands"
and you are living in a big city, Lauren,
where you must wear shoes all the time.
I wanted to speak
and tell you what "almost" means.
I almost died
but today I am alive.
I even forgot to tell the landlady, at least to warn her about
that lamp's possible danger to others.

I feel like something happened which changed me
and no one even noticed.
I almost died.
Would it be the same if I had?

Except that I wouldn't be sitting
here writing this. No one understands
why I cut my arms with razor blades
many years ago. No one ever understood that I did not want to die, cut
only the fleshy parts of my upper
arms which did not even bleed a lot.
That I did not want to be hurt, either,
and used a razor blade so that I felt
almost no pain. But I wanted those
scars on my arms, one in the shape
of the first letter of a man's name, so
that I could show on the outside what
the inside of me was like; that I was
marked by an experience I'd had, one
that seemingly almost no one had
noticed.

Indifference. No, lack of a sense of
the weight of seemingly small things.
I cannot bear that.

I write this for you, Lauren,
because I know you are suffering,
and that practically no one is noticing,
or at least they're predicting
that soon you won't feel that way.
But it *is* important.
That it happened.
That it means something.
I didn't die when I touched that lamp two days ago.
Maybe, I couldn't have.
Physically.
But perhaps I could have.
And no one really seemed to notice.

I keep thinking there should be a moon tonight,
for I remember an image from childhood poetry
of the moon,
a cool slim woman, walking in silver shoes,
leaving a trail of silver,
leaving the small shoes themselves,
like comets,
at her door.
And the delightful idea
of dimes
in a little pair of shoes.
Rubber shoes could have saved me.
But it was summer.
And I was barefoot.
And I didn't die after all.
No one really knows that I will never touch a lamp again
without thinking
of how
unthinking we all always are
about the invisible current that often passes
through our friends,
and we not noticing

                because,

                        after all,

they *didn't* die.

Virtuoso Literature For Two And Four Hands

Nothing is simple or innocent any more
except poetry and music.

I.

Memory relies on emotion.
No other part of the mind does.

A night near New Year's Eve, in New York City.
I do not remember if it was raining,
but it was either cold or damp,
weather that affects you like someone tracking mud
onto your freshly scrubbed kitchen floor,

and my life was falling apart,
that is
the man I loved was running away from me
as if I were a
leaking ceiling or a broken step, and he,
a homeowner, fatigued,
eschewing one more repair.

A party in a prosperous uptown apartment
was something to do,
voices, faces, fragrant and effulgent,
like gardenias on a hothouse tree,
forced in a December greenhouse,

the story of that night is a story of waiting,
a story of waiting for a hand which was not there
to touch me on the shoulder and say, "Let's
go home," a story of waiting
for a carpenter in a land where there are no
trees, a story of waiting,
waiting,

except for one moment which I remember,
like an afterimage from bright light:
a man,
an old friend,
a writer and teacher,
sat down at the piano/   he was drunk and nostalgic,
and bending over the keys like the limbs of a willow,
he played "Stella By Starlight,"
here in this company of intellectuals and poets,
he forgot where he was.
He forgot the rain and the evening of talk,
and played as if he were in some 1940s piano bar,
a song none of us knew the words to,
here in this company of intellectuals and poets
he played "Stella By Starlight"
this man who read Blake and Reich and Vallejo,
who listened to Bruchner in his spare time,
who did not believe in popular art,
even Bob Dylan or the Rolling Stones whom we all listened to.
He sat there
and with reverence
played "Stella By Starlight"
And I remember that part of the evening better than anything
else.

Though I later went to a jazz club and heard exciting Pharaoh
Sanders,
though I later sat desperately with a man who asked me
why,
why I was faithful to that man I loved,
the one who wanted nothing to do with me,
and I could not answer.
I could not answer.

II.

I could not answer,
because the simple answer,
the true answer,
was one I could not believe.

> Nothing is simple or innocent any
> more, except poetry and music.

A night near Thanksgiving,
in Wisconsin, snow crystals blowing through the air,
an owl in the nearby woods
reminding me that I am alone,
"a woman alone"
(my mother always referred to herself as "a woman alone"/
I learned it was a desperate and terrible condition).
I visit friends.
They too have a piano in their living room,
gleaming in the dark, like brandied cherries
in a flat french bottle.

Whenever my life falls apart, I am reminded
that I still have not fallen apart.
The owl, speaking alone in the woods, the one
we never see; we know he is waiting for a small soft creature
like a mouse, to snap the backbone in half,

                                    and that this
is not cruel but simply his means of sustaining life.

The piano glows in Mary and Walter's living room,
the luster of the wood is like well polished boots
promising the hands and feet someplace to go.
I feel the energy of the piano and remember my old friend,
writer and teacher,
who sat down and played,
so lovingly,
"Stella By Starlight"

                    sun
                    moon
                    stars
                    minerals and fire which liberate us from
                    earth & water
and I tell them my meager story,
wondering why we are not satisfied with our minds
unless our hands can do their share.

As if in a story, myself,
I tell them of my promise when I was twenty-one
not to touch the piano again,
to take the motion of my hands
and transform it
into the energy of my life,
and then I confess that I feel the piano vibrating in the next
room, like a nova, an exploding star, one whose heat and light
I cannot resist,

16

and I go in to the piano with my hands on fire
and sit down and play old Chopin preludes/   my fingers have
not touched the keyboard for fifteen years,
they do not respond automatically,
but they remember patterns, they remember rhythms,
they remember chords and keys,
and they do not wait,
they do not wait,
they touch the keyboard, I sway, bending my body like a willow
tree, one which will weep for me.
I do not know "Stella By Starlight" but I know Chopin,
and I let my friends hear me,
how badly I play now
I remember the pleasure of touching

                          sun
                          moon
                          stars
                          that owl lonely in the woods
                          obsidian and ivory
                          the hard rocks of life

they did not ask me
why
I do not play, why I am faithful to my promise
though touching the keys means so much
to me,
They knew I could not answer,
or rather,
that I could
but that my answer
would not be an
answer.

III.

Nothing is simple or innocent any more,
including poetry and music?

> My friend, the astronomer, cannot rec-
> ognize the constellations in the sky.
> They are not math or science.
> He honors truth,
> not poetry.

A night in spring,
Colorado mountain air, like razors near the cheek,
my husband and I entering a mountain resort bar,
a place where they serve beer in half-yards, steak and kidney pie
  is on the menu,

> the entertainment is an old lady
named "Juneau Hattie" who plays ragtime piano.
We sit among business men and college boys,
someone from Sigma Chi having a birthday,
middle-aged tourists drunk and revealing marital fears,

> "My mother was afraid I would marry the first man in
> uniform who came along . . .

> and I did"
drinking Irish coffee,

> thin and steamy against the cold night
outside.
We are together and happy.
My hands move along with the piano player's hands.
She is thumping out
"My Wild Irish Rose," "Take Me Out To The Ball Game,"
the exposed hammers above her keyboard moving
the way they must move every night for her.

She is over fifty, wears a green silk dress, Hong Kong style, slit
up the sides; and a little green hat she may have made herself.
Thin legs, like sticks, under a chunky body. Spindly arms
that hammer out tunes we members of the bourgeoisie can sing
together.
I think of her playing every night, every night having
to be gay, a party, wondering how she can do it,
knowing that we all
always
are on stage,
that we all do it,
though each day gets harder.

How can she bear to play those same songs every night,
put the same emotion into them?
My friend and I,
the man who played "Stella By Starlight," and I, who was moved
to confess to the keys my longing for them last winter,
could we be moved
more than once?
He,
had he played "Stella By Starlight" any time in the past ten
years?
Will he again,
in ten more?
I,
holding my hands away from the pianos I have passed,
like a hiker in the hot dry mountains refusing to open his can-
teen of water until he is absolutely sure he could not continue
without it,
taking a sip,
and saving the rest for another
desperate time,
I yielding that one night to Chopin in winter

and knowing that I would not be so tempted again
for at least fifteen more years . . .

Drinking Irish coffee, listening to this music-hall performer
who probably makes little more money than will pay her rent,
buy her Irish whiskey;
                            sitting with a man I love,
one who cares for me,
wondering how
we renew
our emotions each day,
wondering what it means to have a simple desire
with a simple response.
                            Nothing is simple or innocent any
                            more, except poetry and music.
When I speak,
I hear many other voices,
like a tv store with the sets all tuned to
different channels,
When I listen,
I no longer can identify voices,
often
do not know the words of songs,
cannot remember
the names of
pieces.
When I type the word "piano"
my fingers often slip.
They spell "pain" Oh,
how do we do it?
                    Get from day to day,
when nothing is simple or innocent,
not even poetry or music?

The Woman Who Tap-danced

In the room next to the office where I sat, there was someone who loved a man named Ravel. You could hear the
arpeggios rippling through the walls, as if water were running
over fresh vegetables in the sink—green scallions, carrots firm
and cool to the teeth, lettuce curling like steel springs and
leeks fat and thick as a country girl's white ankle.

The leafy notes of the piano followed one another with the
profusion of crocus and lily of the valley on an earthy spring
hillside. My ears followed, as my eyes will not stay away
from the colors of hyacinth and daffodil. I even felt the full
smooth notes against my ear, as if I were touching a tulip
against my face. It was difficult. I was trying to concentrate on
poetry, and instead I heard the music of a man named Ravel
moving through my walls, an ocean against cliffs,

On the wall, the sun projects the patterns of a venetian blind,
looking like a paper skeleton from the dime store that
attached paper bones with fan-folded crepe paper.

Tonight I heard a Chopin nocturne on a phonograph in a
shabby restaurant with pretensions of gentility. Imagine pretensions of gentility in 1974.

The woman who tap-danced was living in a borrowed apartment above a poet. Imagine how much better it would
have been if the apartment had been above the borrowed
world of a composer. At least for her. Who tap-danced.

Offering To Trade Lives With The Clam

I met a clam on the beach one day. Obvious. That the place
one would meet a clam, would be the beach. However, I have
had some strange encounters in my life—the zebra on city
streets, the birds of paradise in my luggage, the armadillo in a
Paris bathroom, the okapi in a nightclub in Tangiers . . . Any-
way, it was hot and I was getting wet in the breakers, then
wandered into a tidepool where I met him, standing, smoking a
cigar. As I passed, he quoted Wallace Stevens at me,
            "One must have a mind of winter"
he started to say. I smiled a frosty smile, because I don't like
to talk to strange men, even on the beach, but always
feel a little foolish about this prudery on my part.

I said that Wallace Stevens was one of my favorite poets, and
it was nice to hear that someone in this god-forsaken country
read poetry now and then. I was sure that I had entered a world
where poetry had been abandoned with the Rain God. He
never said anything more, however, though I stood there
for about twenty minutes, for the first time in my life, really
wishing this stranger would talk to me. Especially since he
had a mustache and seemed that he might like intellectual
women.

But he never said another word to me. And I walked on; lay
down in the sun to gather its rays into my body, making the
most of summer and vacation. To be alone is to understand
winter, the snow, contraction, silence. The mind of winter is
always there to guard us from the sun gods and their messengers.
This is not a poem; it is a statement about life. I write it
with the wrists of winter, with ice in my fingers, with the
frost of my passionate lips.

The Neighbor's Cat

wanders into this cool room where I am typing
a letter.
It is skinny & ugly,
like all the cats in this town.
I dreamed last night of a cat
that was fat as a jar of black olives
and had big round eyes like an owl.

I carried the olive cat
into the kitchen;
it yelled at the little skinny one   who

                                        was pissing

on my floor;
I found I had no voice left,
but it didn't matter
since my olive cat was doing all the yelling
for me.

Sometimes when I wake up,
in the morning,
I think for a minute
I have lost my voice
and will never speak again.
Then that damn cat wanders into the room,
as I lie against the rough white sheets,
and I yell, "Get out of here;
you make me sneeze"
knowing for sure then,
you always have your voice
when there is something
you really need
to say.

Poem Beginning With A Line From A Zebra

this country, with diamond borders & glass places
keeps me wandering.
I cannot find
my own mailbox
                    Is it
between the paws of two lions
                              Is it
an abandoned piano in a warehouse
                                    Is it
a suitcase
a reminder
that I am a traveller,
                    riding
my hippogriff
              I cross your desert
every day
on my way to work.
                    Now
all life is familiar
whether arranged in Tiffany's
or at Remington's
                    (my favorite bar)
Hello
I say to myself
alone
every morning
              and think about how
none of us understands
each other's life.

Story

A man asked me
what the story of my life was.
I said
I had no
story.
That my stories were all lives,
like mushrooms,
seeming to have no roots,
though the spores, microscopic, dancing over the ground
the way my hand brushes your face when you
are asleep,
          are not mysterious any more;
and I remembered that all stories are one story,
leaving a woman with a handful of silver
that turns to moonlight
slips away as air,
disappears with the sun,
she standing with her own hands open
and poetry which is music,
a song which haunts us all
is what she has left,
her reality mysteriously,
perhaps microscopically, gone
                    to appear in some other patch
of damp ground.
I look for the magician who understands
what is invisible
to the naked eye,
who reads poetry as a text
for a new kind of garden,
who turns moonlight

into a handful of silver,
something solid and real,
not the illusion,
not the old stories,
not the old version of life,
not mushrooms as poisonous toadstools.

Mushrooms,
edible,
beautiful,
dropping their spores,
passing their lives on
just like the rest
of us.
The story of my life
is that
it goes on.

The Bouquet

of blood/
           on the street.
I know what it is,
saw the man fall
(from his bicycle when his child stuck his shoe in the spokes),
saw his neighbor,
the lady who wanted to help,
bring out the roll of paper towels, thinking
         to wipe up the blood from the asphalt
                  after the ambulance left/   but
giving up her purpose
knowing she meant to wipe away memory, perhaps.

I saw the ambulance leave, carrying him
with the flesh and bone gone from his nose,
the blood covering one eye as if
in some child's coloring book, a 3-year old had scribbled red
over a raccoon's face,
and I sat in a foreign household and watched a neatly clad
housewife bring out her roll of paper towels,
thinking to wipe up the blood off the street.

What restrained her?
I wonder.
        Knowing there was so much there
perhaps?
A pool so big,
the parodying of all those tv ads—"It's absorbent!" and "Mrs.
Suburban Housewife, tell all of our listeners now
just how absorbent it *is!*"

27

"You wiped up a whole pool of blood spilled on the street!"

"Now that is something, isn't it!"
all you listeners out there,
and the exclamation points follow everything,
remember you can wipe anything away
with paper towels.

But what impressed me,
the voyeur,
the foreign visitor to this American suburb,
was that this housewife walked out, with her roll of paper
towels, and then she silently,
almost stealthily, put them behind her back,
   —ashamed, I wonder—
and walked back into her house
without using them.
The pool of blood too big?
No, not for the absorbent towels.
Perhaps some sense of history
that you cannot wipe a man's blood from the pavement
when his child has thrown him there.
                                                The bouquet
of blood
blackens,
wears itself into the street,
the stain a reminder
of a simple deadly
accident.

Of life.
I remember the simple dignity
of the neighbor,
the housewife who wanted to help,
bringing out her roll of absorbent paper towels
and then not touching the pool of blood,
refraining from wiping up a man's blood as if it were some
sticky mess
   her kids dropped on the floor.

Daily life dulls us.
Going to the office,
cleaning up the messes of others,
and yet some sensitivity was left to this woman.
She understood, looking at the pool of blood scraped out of the
man
her neighbor's face, as if he had been strip-mined by some ex-
ploiting industrialist,
she knew that she could not just wipe his blood from the street
with her paper towels.
She understood history,
memory,
record.
And I will not forget her,
a common housewife,
who rose above her nature.

Cobra Lilies In The Supermarket

for Wallace Stevens

I wonder
as I am driving to the Market Basket
why I have lived my life
as I have.

The mother of
my third husband
        —a blond blue-eyed singer, she was—
told me
I was a crybaby
because,
at the time,
I was crying.
She said
you should fix up your life
and then not cry
about it.

My own mother
said, referring to my fourth husband
                    who left me
"What are you crying for?
Buy your own house so that the next one who leaves you
won't be able to take your home away."
And she too said,
"You always were
a crybaby."

When I cry now
it is usually in anger. But
sometimes
I still cry in pain. Then I hide myself in rooms where no one
can see me.
I bought a house
but cannot live in it.
My fifth husband says he would leave me
before living there,
and since he is a nice man
(or perhaps it is just that I am older)
I didn't cry,
nor have I recently been called
a crybaby.

I still live in other people's houses,
listen to their music,
live out of suitcases.
Driving to the supermarket in the rain today,
shopping for someone else's dinner,
I wondered if anyone ever felt
he had a home
other than in his head.

I was tantalized with the cobra lily sitting next to the oranges
& avocados like a purple clenched fist
unrolling its tongue
but unwilling to speak to me, I thought.

When I studied the piano
I always cried at my music lessons.
My teacher stopped criticizing me.
I heard that secretly she called me
a crybaby.
I gave up piano
Took up voice instead.
Now,
my lessons are concerts
where crying is considered an art.
I shout,
I speak,
I whisper,
and at last again
I can cry.
This time
no one taunts me
but other crybabies;
and when I am alone
I defend myself with poetry:
"I remember the cry of the peacocks."

The Emerald Essay

This is the third of a group of "poem lectures" which I have been writing on the general theme *form is an extension of content*. This piece is about the use of image. It was originally written for the Boatwright Literary Festival at the University of Richmond in February 1973 and first published as one of my columns ("The Craft of carpenters, plumbers, and mechanics") in *The American Poetry Review*.

I originally wrote the piece because I was asked to give a talk on "What Women Are Up To" and I felt that once and for all I wanted to make the statement that women are up to the same things men are up to. I use the letter format for these poem lectures because I want them to be as personal as a letter, even though they are addressed to formal and abstract subjects.

*   *   *

Dear DAVID & ANNETTE,

my most civilized friends, who remind me that there will
always be a serious audience for serious art, and that they are
both part of the good life, seriously critical of the world,
as well as being serious rejoicers in it,

I have been asked to talk about the subject of what women
are up to, today, and have chosen to ignore the social implica-
tions of that question and address myself to the subject of
poetry as an extension of life, and to the subject of art because
I am an artist.

I have spent the three days I have been here looking with
fascination at the gigantic emeralds ringed with tiny diamond
studs that Katherine Anne Porter wears on her pale bird-
like hands. One, the smaller one, is shaped like a large tear-
drop and I think of these southern catalpa trees that now
in winter are bare with sexual pods hanging from the limbs like
walking canes, and how in a few months they will be covered
again with heart-shaped green leaves/   like the green tear-
drop emerald on Katherine Anne's little finger of her right hand,
a leaf seen through the rain or floating on some swollen stream.

And then there is the Big Ring. A square or perhaps I
should say rectangular one, an emerald that extends to her
knuckle, that reaches over the sides of her middle and little
fingers on her left hand, like the green awning over a porch, a
stone you could look into and see a past of exotic fish swimming
in it, or the future/   the canals of Mars, and the tiny diamonds surrounding it like commoners flocking to see the
Queen of England.

These emeralds fascinate me. I can feel their substance which
is part of their beauty, can fantasize a handful of them, as
if I were holding a handful of dripping wet seaweed at the
beach, or I had reached my hand into a sack or barrel of grain
and were letting the cool smooth kernels touch my closed palm,
or I were holding my own long silky hair in my hand, feeling it as if it were part of a silk drape. But their beauty and
substance, which tantalize me, are not what obsesses me. I
have thought about Katherine Anne Porter's emeralds for the
past three days because they are symbols of her success as a
beautiful woman and an influential writer.

Peter Taylor told me, when I asked about the emeralds, that she had bought them with some of the handsome profits from *Ship of Fools*. Whether this is true or not is irrelevant. For me, they are symbols of the fact that women as writers are up to the same things men as writers are up to—that is, converting the imagination into something tangible and beautiful, big for its size and yet so small we can wear it on our two hands; that artists are like women in that when they receive wealth, they turn it into something beautiful to look at, small and yet magnificent in its surroundings. The emeralds themselves make the diamonds surrounding them mere background. They are symbols, images, and metaphors of their own reality. They are what comes out of life, not life itself.

When I have been tired or bored and feeling the need for poetry, for the last three days, I have looked for Katherine Anne's emeralds. When the conversation has flagged, I have mentioned Miss Porter's emeralds. When I have felt that we have talked too much about art and poetry and not been living it, I mention her emeralds. "Have you seen her emeralds?" I have said to everyone. Not have you read her books (because everyone has read her books) but, "Have you seen her emeralds?"

These emeralds, surrounded by diamond chips, remind me of a set of dreams I had when I was in college in the '50s. I had a series of dreams, night after night, which I called my green silk dreams, and which I recorded each day. In them, green represented poetry, and the floors were always draped with huge fine bolts of green silk; they were unusual dreams because each night they continued, like a serial story, and of course the green silk was the dominant fact of them.

35

At that time, a roommate in the apartment several of us students lived in had a green paste ring which looked like an emerald. She used to let me wear it when I read poetry or painted little watercolors because I said that when I looked into it I could see a secret room, also green, in which my fantasies were played out. I have not been able to look at Katherine Anne's emeralds without thinking that she must sit alone with her feelings often and look into the liquid of those pieces of rock and visualize her fantasies also. Without fantasy, real life is incomplete and dull. Without some substantial real life, there is no fantasy possible.

Images are a way of shaping poems. I do not mean using images to decorate poetry. I mean images as icons. Images as the structure, the bones, gleaming behind the flesh. Katherine Anne's emeralds this week have been the structure on which I have tried to hang my flesh.

I like gleaming images. Here is a list of gleaming black things which I have used in poems:

> eels
> leeches
> grand pianos
> watermelon seeds
> patent leather
> obsidian
> my black velvet coat
> a Doberman pinscher
> oil bubbling out of the ground

Women have always been the interior decorators rather than the architects. I would like to propose that the image which used to be decoration in poetry is now becoming the building, the room itself. I would like to propose that Katherine Anne's emeralds are a room she's built and not a decoration on her fingers.

Let me tell you a story which is an obsession with me. I lived
with a man, a mechanic, who was always covered with grease.
I loved him very much. He had a Doberman pinscher with a
gleaming black coat and clipped ears who lived with us, who
was vicious and bit people though she loved them. This Doberman loved to look at herself in the bedroom mirror and, in
fact, pawed a hole in the rug in front of the mirror over the
years, looking at herself, black as obsidian, in the mirror. I loved
this dog very much, and when the motorcycle mechanic left
me to live alone in the woods, he took his Doberman with
him. But she apparently bit everyone who came to his cabin,
and he finally had to shoot her.

He loved his dog but hated her dependence on him. I am
sure he shot her himself and did not take her to the pound. I
am sure that it broke his heart, but that he also liked shooting
her. The image of this rugged man with a mustache and power-
ful shoulders who had lived with me and rejected me,
shooting the Doberman pinscher whose body shone black as
Chinese lacquer, is one that haunts me and appears in my
mind every time I see a jewel, like Katherine Anne's emeralds.

I spent many months thinking about the look on the dog's
face when she was hit with the bullet and the look on the man's
face as he shot her. I spent a day last November walking on a
beach by a lake which was covered with a thin layer of snow,
walking in shiny black boots and wearing a black velvet coat,
soft and shiny as a seal, with a red bandana sticking out of the
pocket and wondering about these images, knowing that I could
not really connect them, but still knowing that somehow they
were a structure, a connection.
The Doberman, black as caviar,
my coat, soft and black, like a panther,
my boots, crunching the sand,

the black muzzle of the gun—they blue the barrel/ powder
burns are black
the red that must have appeared in the hole as the bullet pene-
trated the dog
my final understanding that love is not something that goes
away, nor anything which prevents pain or even that can be
lived with, that this man in his black leathers, riding his Vincent
Black Shadow or his BSA Gold Star into the night, was the
Prince of Darkness, the Ishmael I loved,
                    Motorcycle Mechanic
                    Woodsman
                    Plumber
and that the pain of losing him is an image that itself must
be a structure in my life, and that I love another man now, the
man with the silver belt buckle, the elusive King of Spain as
well, and he is also a structure composed of images. That a
myth is a set of beautiful memorable images we string together
with different narratives each time. That the constellations in
the sky exist as stars which we outline into shapes with our
pencils, imaginary lines as exciting to us as the stars themselves,
but that the stars are the structures, the images are the
skeleton, that concept rests in the image, that "there are no
ideas but in things."

Let me tell you how poetry is mythology. And mythology is
image. When I was in California for the summer in 1969
and very much alone, pining for the motorcycle mechanic, I
met a man who had nothing dark in him at all. He was golden,
as only Californians can be golden. The first time I saw him,
I felt like he came out of a fairy tale. I found out who he was
and haunted the place where he worked to talk to him. Actually, I did not like talking to him. I liked looking at him. But
I was still in love with the man in leathers, the motorcycle
mechanic. Ironically, the golden man cared even less about me

than my betrayer. But, in my poems, I began to imagine a man like the golden one whom I called the King of Spain. He was a mystery. Never quite there. Yet mysteriously appearing and disappearing in such a way as to make me know he followed me wherever I went. The next year, a man whom I only met for a few hours one evening fell in love with me and began to fantasize that he was the King of Spain. When I met him again this year, I told everyone I had found the King of Spain. I even wrote a poem called "Discovering the King of Spain."

After a day, I told him that I was going to meet The Man With The Silver Belt Buckle, and for days I would allude to going off to meet The Man With The Silver Belt Buckle. He too became a mysterious, missing, desirable character in my poems, who loved me but was never there. Last week I sent the King of Spain a silver belt buckle as a present.

After looking at Katherine Anne Porter's emeralds all week, I have decided that perhaps I would now like to find the man with the emerald ring.

Here is a little story about The Man With The Emerald Ring:

> Once there was a man whom all women fell in love with. He was invisible, except for a huge emerald ring which he wore on his right hand, on the ring finger. The ring was so large that the husbands of beautiful women whom the man with the emerald ring visited always noticed when he was there. It was hard for them to accuse their wives of infidelity when their rival was an invisible man. However, that ring flashed in and out of their lives in such a way as to make many of them more furious than when a certain handsome mustached young poet used to visibly visit their beautiful wives, sitting on the verandas at five, drinking martinis.

39

How's that for the beginning of a story?

Before I go on, I think I'd like to try out another beginning:

> A poem is a story in which the images are more important than the narrative. Once there was a man who became invisible because no one loved him. However, he had a magnificent emerald ring which everyone could see. Whenever he went anywhere, he caused consternation, as everyone could see the giant emerald, like a frog, wet from the pond, sitting in the middle of the room.

Or how about this:

> Once there was a woman who was in love with a man who wore an emerald ring on his finger. However, she could not speak because she had a begonia in her mouth instead of a tongue, and when she tried to tell the man with the emerald ring that she loved him, petals fell out, but no words were formed.

Perhaps if the story begins with the emerald ring, it could be hidden in a sugar bowl in the house of a midget or a scholar of Urdu.

> Once there was a girl who lived with a Doberman pinscher and who fell in love with a shooting star. She wore an invisible emerald ring.

How can I tell you a story when I cannot decide on a good beginning? I know what the ending is, though: A statement about poetry.

The poem is the image
It gives us some beauty to live for both
when life is good
and when it is not.

This week I am obsessed with Katherine Anne's emeralds.
Have you seen her emeralds, I keep saying. Have you seen those
magnificent emeralds?

That *is* what women are up to.

> yr friend,
> DIANE

The Liar

Only a rosebush
and a stack of firewood
broken with intent and an axe
lie between me
and another world,
                    one ringed with trees,
that I can't even see,
don't even know about,
another house full of histories and characters.

Is there any way of knowing
who is there
and if it is you?
or if it is someone who in ten years
                              could be
you
In geometry, it always took me longer
than the others
to prove a theorem/   I, wanting to know/   all the possible
routes
        (Roots?)

Still Life: Michael R., Silver Flute and Violets

for M.R.

As if I could remember you still for a moment,
always moving,
like a fountain that passes and repasses
the same water,
keeping sparkling and pursed
against the metal lips
which shoot and crackle it

And violets coming
into the room where you are standing,
though that gesture for you takes up many
square feet of space,
held in the hand of a girl
who was herself fragrant and intense,
violet against the wet woody ground, was violet
against brown damp trunks

And you reading poems by a man
who probably broke his neck against the green scummed water
in a deep well,
        Green,
        I want you green,
        Green wind,
        Green branches . . .

*   *   *

There is a small nut of life in me
that is never touched
by life around me.
I am myself moved, in retrospect,
by how little I've had, and how not understanding
the extreme poverty of my life
left me innocent
of the worst thing poverty does to people/
                                        bitterness.

*   *   *

Well, my friend,
you did not have your music lessons
when you were young.
And I had mine, though at a price.
And neither of us
is a musician today, though we have each spent
a decade of time practicing our hands against our ears
and we understand measured cadences better than most other
speakers can.
And neither of us can give up poetry or music
as emblems.
You carry your silver flute everywhere,
and a small wooden one in a case by your side.
And I my mythical piano
which makes my shoulders rounder each year.
Weight
of the past . . .
Who is the girl holding the bunch of violets?
For she was only an emblem
when my hands were still bloody
                            from the keys.

The Inevitable Garden

for S.A. who understands my music

Even poetry
and a yard of bare dry earth
yielded fruit and flower
to the imagination
>   iris like jade carvings
>   sweet pea of summer, like bumblebees and
>   oysters
>   the apricot, as smooth as the cheek
>   of a beautiful woman

With a few patches of mowed weeds for a lawn
I lived till I was eight,
surrounded by citrus groves,
the oranges glowing on the trees like swarms of lightning bugs
at night
and a victory garden with sweet little carrots.
We had a skinny rosebush
all thorns
with many new leaves/   the color of a young girl's nipples.
It bore at least three fragrant white roses each year.
And honeysuckle tried to climb in through
our broken windows.

In my black high-topped shoes
(for I had weak ankles)
I would sit on the steps
at seven-year-old dusk
with my child's cardboard trunk
of pencils and paper,
my book of poems,
                    "Silver Pennies"
and think of everything beautiful
I knew.

I wonder where we get our faith in life?
when "Let's Pretend" radio theatre and Grimm or Anderson
are so much more real?
Perhaps one source for me was
                    the lantana hedge next door visited by monarchs
                    and swallowtails,
                    the large lemon-and-black spiders around the
                    edges of the house,
                    the rosebush—for it occasionally budded and
                    flowered,
                    even poor nights
                    were fragrant
                    with night-blooming jasmine,
                    honeysuckle
                    and orange blossom,

They're just the inevitable garden I knew at seven
in a land too far south for apple trees,
though we had
pomegranates there,
and tomatoes.

Oranges, of course.
Birds-of-paradise
were common flowers.

Walking Past Paul Blackburn's Apt. On 7th St.

I wanted to take a walk
and think of the city
whose only remaining beauty
is that you wrote about it.

I bought an ounce
of Carpathian mushrooms from the mountains
of the Ukraine
in the store beneath your old
apartment
       Paul, for you,
       these gestures:

I walked into the store,
seeing in the window a string/   many strings
of powdery white mushroom caps,
brown-gilled underneath, among the amber
and big crocks of honey, nestled next
to embroidered ribbons of purple green red
yellow and blue, simple
puffed blouses and thick books with gold letters.

"How much for a string of mushrooms?" I
innocently asked.

Wonder. Awe.
       "A string?" A pause.
   "We sell them by the ounce,
     and they are light as a feather. But a string—
     $30 maybe?"

"I'd like an ounce then," and he put them in
a tiny paper bag which might have also held a
child's glove
or a marshmallow.

He smiled and told me how delicious they were;
how they would swell up and fill a soup,
how choice they were—only the caps

Paul, I walked out
thinking how you have taught all of us
to dwell in this city and
to make friends with our neighborhoods.

Hello, Paul, I hope you have
found the ultimate
city.
Or maybe you have wisely moved to the country
in your old age?

A Poem With A Blackburnian Warbler's Beginning

under yr,
I mean,
in yr,
what I mean to say is,
on yr,
no,
   I was thinking of walking a trail by a creek in Texas
where I saw
first
snowdrops,
then iris,
then wild cherry blossoms which smelled like
tortillas,
then narcissus and I bent down
several times
to pick them,
thinking of the bare hotel room
I was staying in,
and of how a spray of forsythia,
a branch from cherry or plum,
a blue violet
would give me some sense of my life
different from the institutional walls
but each time
I stopped my hand,
knowing that my pleasure
was in coming upon these colored occasions
in their bare spring settings
and that to pick
was to
    contradict
what my pleasures were about.

50

I bent many times,
trying to make the gesture,
each time taking out my pocket knife,
then always thinking,
no, Diane,
those flowers belong here
in these woods

Going home to the hotel
and meeting a man who sold flowers
on the way,
again not buying or taking any flowers
but standing for half an hour in the wind
just wanting to be near him,
perhaps because he had the flowers
and I also knew they were not mine

I think of your lips
under your mustache
like a baby walrus who might be born this time of year,
spring,
and the surprise of finding them there,
the pleasure,
the stopping to surrender to the landscape,
and how I bent wanting to take you with me,
into my head,
my life,
my suitcase,
everywhere I go,
and how I stood around for an hour in the wind,
just to be near
                    what?

you?
yr lips?
some sense of beauty?
some affirmation of life?
This is
a letter
from the huntress
to the sailor,
wanderer,
seeker.
      I have
the sun
in my heart,
the moon
under my slipper,
and I will never pick the snowdrops
down by the river.
I will give you all the riddles
I have tied
into my hair,
          I shake it loose
watch
something will fall out
A star?
A flower?
The rain?

Yr lips? Have they been hiding
all this time
on the nape
of my neck?

Tango-ing

As If The Ballet Russe Would Ever
Have Looked At My Square Body And
Funny Feet

This man
is tall and slim
and confesses   that at twelve
                        dancing school
he could do   all   the steps.
If he had been born wealthy
and lived in the '30s
he might have spent every evening   in   a   tuxedo,
dancing in nightclubs
                  the Flamingo
with a reputation like Nero Wolfe's secretary and sleuth,
                              Archie   Goodwin
for being the best dancer on the floor.

I,
I have dreamed for years of dancing Swan Lake,
for years have mentally lifted my legs and pointed my toes
next to a wooden bar, the mirror a great deceiver
to anyone with imagination,
and it is with chagrin
I look at myself here in real life,
a chunky short peasant with magical square feet
and a fear of my body
which makes me move awkwardly.
For years,
I have dreamed of my other self,

told stories to make her real.
You, apparently too,
like an imaginary life
tango-ing across the dance floor

> Coconut Grove
> The Starlight Roof of the
> Waldorf Astoria

Funny,
for I see you
tall,
slim,
the man who could do those things if he wanted,
whereas you can only see my body
as it is.

Funny,
too,
that you should love me
in spite of my incredible squareness;
And I, you,
for the imaginary which in my mind
is already achieved.

I think of all the dancers I have known,
one leaped out of a window   to his death,
all have lost husbands or wives,
one dances in agony for a set of mutilated, dying intestines,
one showgirl   now drinks rather than dance for no admirers.
What can I say?
That I loved trying to learn to tango with you last night
alone in our dark quiet house,
with me humming the tune & beat?

And that I was glad to sit down laughing at my own clumsiness
ten minutes later,
knowing you did not love me less,
for one more act
I imagined
yet could not perform.

Winter Sequences

The rain was as slight as
the sound of someone's breathing at night.
The day in the mountains pale grey.
We had brought good cheeses,
a Boursin I especially liked,
wine, and a Pinot Chardonnay,
some liverwurst, french mustard,
pears, apples

for a picnic.

But first we hiked a simple circuit trail
which led us through deep mulchy ground.
I found surprising fungi
and didn't have a field guide to identify them by.
Tiny orange balls
on needle stems.
Snowy white puffballs
looking as if some golfer had lost them,
even the old puffballs turning brown,
wearing prickly skins like sycamore fruit.
Step by step, as I walked along
picking out inky caps,
I kept my secret.
First I would ask myself,
could I tell it so that it captured the moment?
No.
Then thinking about it more and more
I just wanted to spill it.
But I've remembered too much about what I've learned
to really spill it.

I hold my secrets.
They are poems only I can read.
In the dark
under the stars.
No, once it is a secret
there is no joy in telling.

Rain cleared one muddy spot on the grass
across from my office.
I walked by it looking closely for mushrooms.
There were none.

Can I tell you now
without sounding like a fool?

The air is so cold it stretches across your face
paralyzing it,
making you think
a hard glue has dried there
and left your face immobile.
The sun is shining as brilliantly on the pyracanthus
as a piano performance of Rubinstein.
The scene could either be a palm-tree-lined street
in Los Angeles
with pink stucco houses, mock orange, and jasmine bushes
or a New England town,
covered with fresh snow
where the crunch of boots shakes
holly wreaths on the porch door.
Does it matter where you find beauty?
that it immobilizes you,
makes you want to stop the passage of time,
makes you define each object
                         Landscape, the most brilliant

and terrible kind of beauty
causing us to remember our mobility
essence of life
and wish we might stand still,
just stand still.

White mushrooms,
as large as the headlights on a car,
Pure white.
Flat as an operating table.

It is precision
that defines beauty.
                    Beauty
is either contrasts or subtleties,
the unexpected
or
the inevitable.   This is a coda
for descriptive information:
not poetry.
White mushrooms.
Three of them, as large as the open lips of
calla lilies.
Their brown perfectly ribbed gills
cool and fleshy,
touching, like the cool skin of someone you love

I kept thinking and holding my secret
to myself
as we hiked that trail
knowing that if as we stopped either in the climax forest
or the field on the other side of the mountain
filled with foggy milkweed pods,
and striped green gooseberries,
that if I said,

>"A few days ago I saw three mushrooms as big as the
>headlamps of cars/
>They were on a lawn across from my office.
>I bent down on my knees to see if they were real,
>and
>touching them
>found they were cooler and softer than skin. A
>dolphin's skin perhaps.
>I thought they were a trick.
>I did not believe they were real.
>Some new plastic, perhaps, invented for rich
>suburbanites.
>I questioned whether they were real.
>I wondered, if they were real, had someone
>planted them there
>to make a fool of me.
>I asked myself whether I should pick them.
>I pondered why, if they were real, no one
>had already
>picked them.
>I bent down and touched them.
>I was almost afraid of them.
>I walked away and did not tell anyone.
>I was afraid no one would understand
>how beautiful they were,
>no, how excited I was.

         I still do not know if anyone can know.
         I still have not revealed
         my secret."
that if I said this,
any one would understand.

When you remember
all the mushrooms or wild fungi
you have come upon by surprise
or
other
sudden-nesses,
a blue crocus
early
anxiously out of the snow,
it is no more exciting
than seeing that red male cardinal
flashing his wings against the snow of winter.
Common,
like arterial blood.
The question becomes
how do we live with the secret of unexpected beauty?

Three cardinal feathers fallen against the snow.
Jonathan's gleaming black dog, Pearl, running in the crystal
park.
My three mushrooms, like the beautiful white hands of the
embroiderer,
growing out of the earth.

The Beautiful *Amanita Muscaria*

for Adrienne who was a piano
prodigy at ten

Warty and common
in Vermont,
yet so brilliant,
like the red-winged blackbirds which have overtaken
midwestern fields,
their epaulets of crimson feathers burn
like fresh blood
on my hand which I cut when chopping
vegetables,
black black
         farmers shoot them
         they are common pests

And the *Amanita muscaria*
a common mushroom,
a scarlet orange with decorator-grey warts
found on any picnic grounds,
so poisonous, you would hallucinate
before you die
yet everywhere

The beautiful things which kill.

Or is it that we are too weak to risk the power
of beauty?
On the porch of my apartment which overlooks a parking lot
I have strewn birdseed.
No birds come,
not even sparrows.

I grew up in a dull world.
It was deadly too.
Not beautiful.   But deadly.

All my life,
I have preached, "You cannot have it both ways"/   you
must choose: virtue or beauty,
comfort or accomplishment,
principle or accord.
And yet, you, my friend, who have beauty comfort and accord
now seem to me
to have far more virtue, accomplishment and principle too,
than anyone.
                    More than I could ever hope for.
A victim of my own notions,
aware of my own sloth and foolishness,
I still preach what I cannot practice,
and have to believe in others
more than myself.
I have given up my piano,
yet yours is still in your living room.

All my life I have questioned my very right to live.
Have never felt I justified any life.
Have worked hard to make myself as interesting to others
as I have, foolishly, always found myself.

What can I say now?
that virtue is in the genes,
that all is unfair,
as I have always protested?

You are born rich or you are born poor?
And the virtuous man
is
the one who kills himself
when he recognizes his lifetime ignominy?

That we are all trying to make ourselves gods,
but that itself is taboo?

The beautiful *Amanita muscaria* was designed for stronger be-
ings than ourselves.
Even with our greatest will
we do not change.

You were the piano prodigy,
and I, untalented,
                    the one who wanted to play.

Driving Gloves

for Anne Winters

I wish my past had been
a volcano,
                spewing me out on a shower of hot sparks,
but it wasn't.
I came from a sad family.
I tried to run away,
and I thought I made the probable
improbable.
But that was a fancy,
a short-lived sweet-pea, climbing up my back fence,
like a girl's summer organdy dress,
worn only once or twice.

Some of their sadness
had to be in me.
Throw these lines away.
Vines that did not flower.

A bud is not a summary.

But it is the total
in a reduced form.

The perverse mimic/   the desire to repeat
whatever's heard
or seen.
The genes,
some big sound studio,
a memory eye,
a stain from Mendelssohn traced through the fluted pea
family.

I learned to drive a car when I was
thirty-two years old. I went back to
California where everyone but me was
driving by sixteen, and, twice that
age, I hired a teacher, hired a car, and
learned to drive. It made me feel free.
I hate clichés, but when you leave
your life alone, there is nothing it can
become, but a cliché. From the
beginning, I insisted on what my
friends considered an affectation. I
wore gloves for driving. I said the
wheel got too hot or cold, that my
hands got sweaty or stiff from rheuma-
tism, that I did not feel in control
without gloves.

In California, almost no one wears
gloves or a hat. They are considered
affectations. Especially in the lower
classes from which I come. Yet, I
remembered this December, while
driving to California from the East
Coast, after four long years of being a
licensed driver, that my mother, improbable as it seems, used to wear
gloves to drive in.

My mother, who went to a one-room
school, who lived in a house with a
dirt floor, who never wore gloves on
any occasion I can remember, who
never wore a hat, who never had any
place fancy to go, who never even
had a job she had to dress up for, she,
she wore gloves when she drove a car.

It is the perverse voice that speaks in us,
going back to old inflections,
old fictional
language of other characters . . .

Your father, Anne,
has written what?
                    ten
unpublished novels?

Surely,
a noble action
we should all admire?
That a man could continue doing for himself
what most of us only do
if the world approves . . .

And he
is a
terrible driver, you say/
disapproved by all the family?
They shudder when he hits the road,
or did you say,
he doesn't have a license any more?

And you're like him
you say?

That's why you are over thirty and letting me assist
in winning your drivers' license?

And you reiterate
how we're all like some parent
or ancestor

But your father also
had four wives,
or was it five?

And you have one husband
a faithful one you would never leave.

And didn't you say your father taught English all his life
to students who had a hard time reading
and writing
and you,
you're a Greek scholar,
a speaker of three languages,
a "bluestocking"
                if we use that term any more
And your only associates are people like me,
all of us finding the illiterate
a painful chore.

Yet,
what are these mimicries that we all look for,
that we fear?

The one thing that has terrified me in the dark
every night of my life
is the thought that I would be like mother,
she, who only read the *Reader's Digest*,
that I would look like her
       heavy and unfashionable,
that I would talk like her
       in a high polite voice
       and worse,
       have nothing interesting to say,
that I would be condemned to a life like hers,
       a sad life,
       discreet of imagination.
But here I am,
unaccountably,
with my driving gloves.

Some stain Mendelssohn found,
like the mole on my left shoulder which has its mysterious twin
somewhere.

You don't want to drive badly, Anne,
or write unpublishable books
or spend your life teaching
the unteachable.

I don't want to spend my life like my mother,
     unable to get along with people, yet convinced that I
     need them,
     working all my life at jobs I hate and which do not pay
     much either,
     insisting that I love everything, anyway,
     claiming to love my children
     parading my sacrifices
     for them.

Talk, talk, talk.
Do we have no courage to live our own lives?
Do we hope the past will live them for us?

No, Anne,
you learned to drive because you are not your father.
And why do I wear these driving gloves?
     because my hands are arthritic?
     because I want to feel like a professional driver?
     because it is a safety measure?
     because my mother did?
No, I wear them, Anne,
because I like to wear them.

Our lives *are* our own.
We must assert it.
We must ask grace from ourselves.
Our memories.
Let them
release us from the past.
What is the past, Anne?

Only something
we have all lived
                    through.

Backing Up, Or Tearing Up The Garden Next To The Driveway

Does it mean anything
that I just can't back up?
My eyes take me forward,
my body not wanting
to be part
             of what is behind
me.
The driveway,
like a scar in life,
the paving left there from former acts,
                              actions,
and I not wanting to retrace
the days, hours, minutes, that made it,
not wanting to go back over
old ground.

But I got my car parked in here,
and turning around
is not possible
on the straight and narrow,
so back I go,
brushing a tomato on one side,
sending pungent crushed fragrance of chrysanthemums
into the air on the other,
a limb off a mock orange,
a wheel mark on the dichondra,
I whisper past the white wooden gatepost
unscratched but scarcely breathing,
resolving always to park on the street from now on,
even though the sign says
                    "2 HOURS"
knowing that I'd rather pay parking fines
than relive a past I don't even consider mine.

History,
your touch,
a memory of a face,
certain hands,
I do not even focus correctly,

reluctant/   reluctant to cover/   all the same ground . . .

To The Young Man Who Left The Flowers
On My Desk One April Afternoon

I accepted them.
                It was the graceful
thing to do, even though I knew
they weren't meant for me:
Far, far too lovely they were—
half blue, wild tolling blue
as lucent and yielding as new
melon flesh and dew, dew on their lips;
half demure, demure and elegant
white rose, sleeping beauties quiet
and masked against any beast.

I cannot say what they meant
to us all, coming at the time
when they did. It was love,
and we opened our hearts,
so much evil having recently skulked about.

They were left, I know, for another girl—
perhaps the afternoon-nymph with unwilting
grace and enormous blue eyes,
so much like those wild, fragrant first flowers
whose heavy perfume I could smell all night,
or maybe it was the white-limbed
marble Greek, smooth as cool Chablis,
whom I found to be so like
those silent tea roses that I gasped
to see perfection in a thing still young;
and yet the flowers pleased me most of all
because I am plain,
and beauty means so much . . .

so very much to me.

A Drab Beach Reminds Me Of A Crippled Woman

her thin short leg
is in a heavy iron brace,
a shoe with a sole like a can of gasoline
on her shriveled foot;
still she hobbles on a cane.
                                    Her skin
is beautiful, pale, an opal or moonstone,
and her husband is dark and quiet.
I'm sure she thinks he's too handsome for her.
She speaks with the voice of a cafe chanteuse,
tries to ignore her big shoe
and the heavy metal around her leg.

I am drinking tea, with two whole legs,
looking at a drab beach,
thinking about all the obvious things,
the inevitable repetitions.

Silence becomes the best remark anyone can make.

Thorny Trunks

green is
the color of

ha,
    you thought I would say life?

but, in fact,
I was simply going to mention
the color of a bicycle
I saw a little boy riding today,
moving along the street
as if
there were a lizard
ten feet tall
behind him,
as if
he had suddenly remembered
it was raining,
though only sun
                    flooded his
face.
I thought of you,
with thorns growing out of
your body,
exotic,
beautiful,
just waiting for me
to press against them.

But you do not understand,
perhaps,
that for me, beauty
is something
which cannot
be touched.

On Seeing Two Goldfinches Fly Out Of An Alder Tree, The Way You Are Swiftly Flying Out Of My Life

4 July 1971. Independence Day.

The grass in this orchard
is newly mown
and lies down
               like children too sleepy to play.

Its scent
oozes into our warm nostrils
My friends are like apple trees
bent in their graceful hospitable forms,
and I love them,
but think of you/
               the hunger
in me
which is open-jawed and broken-toothed
without your presence.
There is no real life for me
when you are gone away.
I become a cataloguer
of life,
listing
the fine smells,
the scent of apple and pine,
even these two goldfinches flying so spectacularly,
so surprisingly,
though there are many

yet each new motion is a discovery
like gold gleaming out of the pan full of rocks,
covered with clear water.

They fly,
gold and black,
out of the afternoon greenness of the tree,
my own eyes not prepared for such loveliness
but my needs,
raw,
a tiger with a ripped bloody shoulder
allow me only to catalogue them
to yearn for the completeness,
some contentment
which can never be in me
without you.

This day,
this sunshine,
these birds,
what a common history we all have.
                              The goldfinches
reminding me
that the natural motion
is to fly
away.

Blessing Ode For A Man With Fishbones
Around His Neck

for H.M.

Armillaria mellea,
honey mushroom,
let it grow by your door
and be edible

Pileated woodpeckers,
tall and handsome,
may they return in abundance
and nest in your hollow tree

Mercury,
the liquid metal,
let your mind follow all of
its forms

May the cow vetch move aside
when you walk in tangled grass

May all the women of the world
show you the shining white insides
of their slender wrists

May the buildings of the world
each be built with a special
room for you

May the shoes of the world
never bind your feet

May your name be spoken
in the places where good mechanics dwell,
be they poets or motormen or carpenters,
for in that company, fame is
a judgment to be proud of

May you never breathe the air
of a place without inspiring
some of the language of its animals,
the forms of its trees and flowers,

May your maps continue to be read
by all serious travellers

This blessing be said
by running water,
near a beam of sunlight,
in the presence of the lady's daytime moon.

Alone, Like A Window Washer At The 50th Story

Now I know
that you must
depend on
some
things.
    A sturdy scaffold,
    a strong harness,
    and your own sense of balance
when you reach the high places.

Do not ever let
anyone hold
these things for you;
do not assume that you will ever
learn to look down
with equanimity.
Do not ask
what others think,
for they are not
doing your job.

I wash the windows,
they sparkle
like the eyes of a snake.

I know challenges,
even when they are not hissing
under my foot.

Now I know that you must
depend
on some things
and I also know
what it is that you have to do
strictly
alone.
All those years
when I was confused
and longed for company,
I was not looking
through the glittering glass,
not knowing the satisfaction
of singular accomplishments,
that windows which are not cleaned
on the 50th floor
look particularly grim,
the grime magnified
by the height;
I alone
restore the beauty, the light.
I am proud,
pleased
to do that
alone.

Buds

Tight and closed
the bud of the rosebush
in my head
has not bloomed yet.

Perhaps
like the bud of a florist's hothouse flower,
it will droop on its stem and die
before it becomes a full flower.

Perhaps it will turn black
Its head will droop.

Seeing the precise petals
furling together
meticulously,
I wish for that excellence,
that perfection in my life.
Knowing nothing
                      about me
could be that well made.

I wonder too,
why it is the drooping that bothers me so much more than the
death.
A full-blown,
yes, that is the word that is used,
full-blown,
a full-blown rose
dries,
crinkles,
but remains upright,
alert,
even when dead,
only the petals becoming papery,
the form not bowing.

But that bud
when it droops
hurts me,
not because it is young
and going.
But because of the way it goes.
Drooping.

I suppose
I know my inescapable
weaknesses.

PS
3573
A42   Wakosi, Diane.
V5   Virtuoso literature for
         two and four hands.

PS3573 A42 V5
  +Virtuoso literat+Wakoski, Diane.

0 00 02 0211015 1
      MIDDLEBURY COLLEGE